STUD BOURNE peeks into a few elements that may have groomed some STUDZ. It describes what it is like to live in a community that, at times, views them through the narrow lenses of fear; religion, and a black feminist microscope. We are a part of a Black lesbian culture that sometimes does not understand us, ridicules us, stereotypes us, admonishes us, and alienates us. However, many of us manage to hold on to our blackness, our spirituality, and to the ones we love.

I have learned that when in battle one can maintain a sense of identity without destroying the armor that shields them, and without taking on too many blows. STUD BOURNE is the voice of one soldier who dares to speak out during the midst of a cultural gender war. Volume One is the first of a twelve-volume collection revealing the true life of Studly Dudly, with Volume Two to be released in late summer of 2008. Finally, I have found the words and have written them as honestly, and as passionately as the heart would allow.

STUD BOURNE

Volume I

STUD BOURNE Vol. I
Author Studly Dudly
© 2008 by D.A. Tunstill
Edited by Helen Lee Khan
Cover art by FIST
All rights reserved by Author and Publisher
ISBN 978-1-4357-1260-7

Contents

Volume 1

Will

For a long, long time I thought that girls were boys who carried their tits on their chest instead of in their pants. I also thought that the reason why boys stood up to pee was because they did not know enough to sit down. Heck, I even tried peeing standing up, but the warm flow of yellow fluid trickling aimlessly down my legs to the floor was puzzling. I could not understand why I was so bad at it; and, why it was so hard for me to hit my mark. Mopping up my wayward streams with gobs of toilet paper, and Mama's constant complaints about its waste made it less appealing.

I tried not to let my failed attempts bother me and truly believed that standing up was a matter of convenience that time, patience and practice would make me efficient. Other than that, I considered myself no different from the rest of the boys in my family. In fact, I ran around with them shirtless on hot summer days, at least until I was eleven.

Back then, I was ignorant of a gender role and it was bliss. Age 11 marked a time in my life when my mother made the decisions to educate me to the ways of women. Now, do not get me wrong; I did girly things I just did not consider them girly. Stuff like cooking, cleaning, and watching Mama getting her hair and makeup together was a magic show to me.

Learning, what it was to be a girl, and to be a female, was not something that had ever crossed my mind. I was already a girl; and being feminine, well I thought that it was a given, even though I had no real clue of what being feminine meant. I was learning to be me after all. I had not begun to think about the role that my gender was all too often expected to play. Being me was all that I knew how to do well. So, why would I feel that it could possibly go against my being a girl? Somehow, I knew that this girl/boy thing held more weight than words. What it held would perplex me until I came home from Grandma's house one day.

My twin brother and I spent the weekend at Grandma's place with our cousins. We had a ball and in our haste to stay overnight, we forgot to bring a change of clothes. We played baseball, football and even terrorized some of the neighborhood kids by playing "Rock Wars." For some of you who did not grow up in the ghetto or poor, let me explain the game of "Rock Wars" to you. "Rock Wars" are snowball fights behind makeshift barriers between neighborhood kids. Now, replace the snowballs with rocks, heat the temperature up, and basically, you got kids hurling rocks at each other in a vacant lot on a steamy summer day with near pinpoint accuracy.

It is a miracle that none of us got more than a few minor scrapes and bruises. Even now when I pass by a vacant lot I can almost recall what the sound of broken bricks, rocks, and concrete sounded like when they whizzed past my ears at fifty miles per hour. After all, those activities coupled with my short knotted fro rendered me rather rough. My brother and I looked like twin bushmen in from a hunt, and when we sat on the *EL* to go home you could see the dust rise from our denim cutoffs.

The haze of dust looked like smoke signals to alert the nearby tribes of our arrival. I was in a state that must have traumatized my mother, because she looked shocked. She stood in the middle of the doorway with her mouth wide open and her hands anchored on her hips. Even though I looked no better than my brother did, I got my ass whipped. Between each lash of the doubled up extension cord I heard my mother yell in her all too familiar Ten Commandment voice, "You are a damn girl!" over, and over, and over again. I felt like one of the chosen people who listened to Moses right before he smashed the laws of God down.

The words that she shouted out took all of the air from her lungs. It was as if she was tapping into a higher source of power by sounding out each syllable as loudly and as clearly as she possibly could. Though I did not recognize it then, I soon came to understand that it was her battle cry. Her voice boomed with the war readiness of a mother who felt that her duty was to pass down the seeds of womanhood to a woman child who clearly did not want them.

The seeds of my mother's womanhood, her mother's womanhood and all of the mothers that came before her were at stake. I knew what she wanted. She wanted a little girl who would play with dolls, a little girl who would not strip off dresses the first chance that she got to go play in the dirt. She wanted to see a reflection of herself. Mama wanted what I could not find in myself to give, and it hurt her to the bone when she saw her little girl looking just like her little boy. This was the very second that I became fully aware of how much my being a roughneck tomboy was affecting her.

Had my mother not screamed at me Moses style, I would have remained clueless as to why she was so pissed. How do you teach someone to be who you want him or her to be? She did not know the answer to that, all she knew was *will*. That same *will* that helped her forgive the rage of her husband. That same *will* that gave her the strength to smile when she wanted to cry. The same *will* that stretched Sunday's dinner into Wednesday's breakfast was being called upon; and, just like before, it would carry her through, even if she had to beat the hell out of me to do it.

This battle, like so many before, was very important to my mother. Instinctively, I knew that I had to stand my ground. I had to fight, and fight hard, or loose who I felt I was. I let my body turn cold and numb as if I were frosty metal in the winter. Nothing could touch me, not even the uncontrollable childhood urge to appease her. So, I stayed still and let the cord cut into my flesh. I was thinking too damn hard to feel anything. Mama's cry roared and quaked with a slight stutter while she repeated her battle song again, and again, and again.

"You are ah… ah… damn girl! You are ah… ah… damn girl! You are ah… ah… damn girl!"

It was obvious that she was uncertain as of how she was going to reshape her child's sacred space, and weave it into a fabric neatly connected to the women who came before.

Maybe that is why I did not do my normal running-in-a-circle dodge-the-ass-spanking routine when she was whipping me. She was mad already, and I could only imagine what she would say or do had I let the words escape from the depths of my soul. Words sharp enough to cut away at thick ancient strands rooted within her own soul while she tried to slice away at mine with every heartfelt stroke. I decided against saying anything. Instead, I planted myself as if I were a twig on a leaf being beat down by the brunt of a forceful wind. I stared straight ahead and stood in the middle of the room, frigid, silent, cold, but inside my head, I was screaming, "But Mama I don't feel like a girl! But Mama I don't want to be a girl and you can't make me!"

Anger swelled up inside of me and I wondered where the fairness of it all was. Eddie was just as grimy as I. So, why wasn't he getting the same ass-whipping as me? Mama stopped swinging and began to search my face. She realized that the daughter who carried her smile, her strength and her will was now using those same birthrights to defy her. Having found what she was looking for and with eyes watering over, she blinked to acknowledge what she saw twinkling in the corners of my own.

What was once considered and analyzed as a phase was not a phase at all. The worries, suspicions and subtle hints had come to a head. A flurry of disjointed thoughts and unanswered questions raced through my mother's mind so fast its force almost knocked her down. She thought, "Is Rhea one of them?" "Was she one of those mannish women?" How would the world view and treat her daughter? How could she have let such a significant obligation get away from her? What would she do with a daughter that hid her femininity under man clothes, man ways, and heaven forbid, man desires? Her child was in a place that she knew nothing of and to which she was completely alien. The power of a mother's influence held little persuasion.

Reaching into her bag of life experience was not enough. Mama was like a novice that had stumbled onto unfamiliar ground. In her mind, she prayed and hoped that her love for me would not lead her astray. I think what startled her most was the glare in my eyes. My eyes mirrored hers, rebellious, fiery and unrelenting.

She had some painful decisions to make and her choices were few. Mama could keep swinging that extension cord and raise a sheep, or let it go and nurture a lion. Slowly, fearfully and bitterly she let the cord slip through her hand and onto the floor. I watched it curl at her feet into a pile of plastic brown licorice.

My mother's last best effort was a trip to the free clinic. I thought that it would be a simple visit for a shot or check up, but it was not, it was for something else. This Doctor did not wear a stethoscope or the white coat with a lollypop in its pocket. This Doctor held a clipboard with a thick yellow pad on it and wore a dark blue suit with black patent leather shoes. Mama said that he was the kind of Doctor who used words to help people.

When she left the room and closed the door, I sat down in the padded tan chair across from the Doctor's desk. The chair made a fart sound as I eased into it. In his pristine white painted office were a wall full of framed diplomas, and a black desk with manila files on top of it flanked by a small sculpture of the human brain. The Doctor smiled at me from across the desk and without hesitation went straight to work. He, who healed with words, let them roll out with the skill of a diamond cutter that shaped gems into fine points. His speech was matter of fact and it held finesse packed with an indifference that caused me to feel near invisible. Yet, I knew that he had to be talking to me because I was the only other person sitting in the room.

"Are you a boy?"

I almost answered him, but could not, because the response was stuck in the back of my mouth like unbaked dough. I did not want to answer him. I did not know him and his questioning left me wondering if I even knew me. Wasn't the soreness of my body an answer? Weren't my silent tears of yesterday's beating enough? Wasn't there enough pain in the air? Couldn't this Doctor who healed with words see it with his own eyes? I felt like I had been shaken from a restful nap. At this point, I would say or do anything to get the pestering to stop so that I could return back to my slumber. I did not want to tell him anything, but I felt the need to hear myself saying the words. I wanted to know what it felt like when they passed through my mind and found their way to the tip of my tongue. I thought, "Who was he to deserve what I did not give my Mama?"

Once more I felt a chill come over me. I felt its ice creep up and freeze beneath my skin; but I stayed silent and allowed the buried bread to bake in my throat. I shook my head in a slight no or maybe yes fashion. I was not sure which, but I did react to his question. "Oh?" He said casually as he jotted down more scribbles onto the clipboard that rested atop his big black desk. He then pushed back his thick-rimmed glasses that had edged towards the tip of his nose, cleared his throat and forged on with more probes.

"Do you like yourself? Do you like your mother? Do you like your father? Do you like your school? Do you like boys? Do you like girls?"

I answered all of his questions, but he never heard a word because I shook my head so much at his probing I doubt that he even knew what I was answering yes or no to.

I did not tell him that boys and girls were the same based on my careful inspections of my brothers GI Joe dolls. I did not tell him how I practiced peeing standing up. I did not tell him how I snuck into the boy's restroom and saw strange toilets with no seats. I did not tell him how I would pray almost every night for God to hurry up and finish his work with me so that people would stop calling me a girl, and Mama would stop putting those ugly dresses on me. I did not tell him how I used to sneak on my brothers underwear because the ones I wore did not have the pee hole in it like his. I did not tell him that I played house once with the neighbors' kids and wound up in the bathroom laying on top of a girl humping her like there was no tomorrow. No, I did not tell him many things I just shook my head yes or no.

Our one-sided conversation continued in that manner. The Doctor chiseled away undaunted by cloaked pieces of what could not be controlled. He was a miner digging well underneath rocks, examining all of the pebbles before tossing away the stones. He slowly and methodically pulled at secrets close to home, and in the process, unwittingly awakened a hidden hibernation that had become bold with every single probe. When the session ended, I was exhausted.

He had a brief private conversation with my mother and then we went home. That was the last time that I saw the Doctor who healed with words. The unpleasant incident between Mama and me never repeated itself and the question of what I was never came up again. Mama went into a silent wait and see mode before taking the cool comfort of a self-imposed closet. Sure, I still got dolls and tea sets for Christmas. Mama still bought me the pink dresses that I never wore seconds longer than I had to, and sometimes we had teatime with Kool-Aid.

Mama held out hope, but she never ever tried to break my will again. Something happened between us. Even though we made no mention of it, we both understood that I would be the Master of my own destiny. She knew and I knew that any attempt to strip me of that God given right would lead us back into war. After all, how could she battle with me for holding on to what she was teaching me to cherish? Her "sticky lesson" of how I felt about myself was far more important than how anyone else did; this time I included her in the mix. In other words, I learned early in life during an ass-whipping to say, "FUCK YOU!" I just did not use the curse words.

Monster

Mama paid more attention to me than usual after our first battle of wills. She took notice of my dread of dresses, dislike of dolls right down to the slightest specks of dirt on my face. I got more love filled spit baths than I could count. My father on the other hand, to me at least, was a monster. I never really liked him. He terrified me because he hurt my mother and there was no forgiveness for his abuse. It did not take too much time for Eddie and me to understand that it was best to stay out of his way; and, just like our first, last and middle names, it was an easy thing to remember.

In the threshold of an open doorway, we saw Mama on the floor. She was next to a toppled end table with father the monster, hovering over her. Mama held the side of her swollen face with one hand and leaned against a ragged plaid couch with the other. Mascara mixed with tears rolled down her face and into the corners of her battered and bruised lips. Drops of blood dotted across her yellow cashier's uniform smock, and long black strands of her hair stood straight up on one end. A tipped lamp lay next to her purse on a brown and white speckled cement floor. Its contents had exploded out and little translucent fragments of a light bulb glowed around loose change and makeup supplies.

"Close the god damn door!" His command rattled me like a weak window blasted by a gust of wind from a strong storm. We inched just inside the door and quickly closed it behind us.

Mama rose from the floor and gingerly sunk into the cushions of the couch. She combed back her pull-string hair, gathered loose strands of it between her fingertips and slowly let them fall to the floor. Eddie ran to her side and leaned on her shoulder. I wanted to run to Mama too, but I could not get my legs to move and wound up standing near the door looking down at her purse then back up at him.

Sweat barreled over my father's butterscotch skin and collected into pools of drool along the edges of his mouth. I looked into his eyes and saw a change in them. His eyes did not have the kind of change that made them a different color. Not the kind of a change that made them bigger, but the kind of change that morphed from a man into a monster then back again. Inside of him was Armageddon, and the heat of its blaze could be felt throughout the whole room.

"Just give me the damn money, Cynthia!" He yelled.

"That's all we got Ed, please don't take it all," Mama said softly as she pointed to her purse on the floor.

He hurried across the room, snatched it up and rifled through it. You could hear the interior zippers rip open as he fumbled through some of its compartments. The last zipper yielded a few pieces of worn paper and he jammed them into his pocket. "Ed, don't take it all," Mama pleaded again.

He stared at her through slits for eyes, then took a bill from his pocket and stuffed it back into her purse.

"Here, damn it!" He scoffed while flinging the purse back at her and storming out of the door. Just as the door slammed, Eddie cried out. The purse hit him in the face and a zipper dug into the soft flesh just above his right eyebrow. The scar it left behind was a visible reminder of the monster's rage for Eddie. Unlike my brother's, my scar went far beyond the skin and a whole lot deeper. My scars went where memories go. I failed to hear Daddy call for me to find his cigarettes and was met with a blinding slap as I sat in our bedroom window daydreaming.

I watched the world from our third floor window with eyes of curious detail. Across the street past the playground, I could see the ladies of the night seduce potential customers and retreat at the sight of slow moving patrol cars. Just a few feet away from them, I could see a one-legged panhandler shaking his rusty coffee can to the beat of passing steps. Down the block, frames of burned and abandoned buildings stood in defiance with the art of angry and artistic youths painted across them. In between the destruction, a few buildings fought to exist, with only the plants and curtains in the windows to give them life. Just below our window, winehead Larry sifted through the dumpster. He mumbled about the quality of trash and how people just don't throw away as much as they used to. In the air, I could smell the bitter smoke of wood burning. The local bums had set a fire to chase away what the alcohol could not. In my ears, I could hear the faint sounds of children crying, and sirens shrieking.

I was close to drifting off into another realm, where the last bits of sunshine changed into silver streaks of moon rays; then, all of the sudden, BAM! Something struck me and it was so quick it stole my breath away. I saw a fleeting flash of lighting and then only black. When I was able to see again, I saw my father's face staring down at me, but it was not his face, it was the monster living inside of him. The muscles in his neck bulged out and his mouth twisted as it moved rapidly, but I heard nothing; nothing but the bells ringing in my ears.

I watched my father like a silent movie and pretended that I could hear his soundless lips. His thick ashen hand marked my face for a while, but no one knew that it was there but me. That is the why my scar went beyond the skin. It was in my head! It was in my ears and very often was the first thing that greeted me each morning. The bells would resonate like internal alarms going off to warn me of imminent dangers. I now strained to hear Daddy's call for his cigarettes "moving to find them like a heat seeking missile."

My father drank a lot, and despite being a diabetic on insulin, he threw caution to the wind. Many times Mama had to make him cups of sugar water to snap him out of a fit. These fits were strange body twisting seizures that landed him on the floor, flopping like a fish out of water and talking gibberish. Mama would rush to the kitchen, stir up some sugar water and make him drink it.

Once Daddy had a fit and Mama sent me to make the water while she and Eddie tried to hold him down. I remember thinking as I rushed to the kitchen and peered back, that they looked like they were riding a roller coaster made of arms and legs, fighting to hang on. Odd as it appeared, there was a normalcy about it that made any fear that I had fade away. Just as Mama taught me, I got a cup, filled it with water and reached for the sugar when something stopped me. I cannot explain my sudden paralysis. So many questions passed through my mind, and for a few seconds I let myself pause on them. What would happen if I put salt in the water? Was it the sugar that brought him back, or was it the sugar that gave the monster life? Would the salt stop the bells in my ears? Would the salt make the monster go away?

"Rhea, hurry up with that sugar water, girl!" Mama's panicked shriek halted my rumination.

"Yes, Mama, I'm coming!"

I do not know how it got into my hands, but I had to put the saltshaker down to grab the sugar. I stirred it into the cup and as the granules circled around the bottom, I rushed it back to her. She snatched it impatiently from my hand and gave me a long scrutinizing look. Her inspection was deep and thorough. I could feel it burrow into me as if something was horribly wrong, then her attention turned back to Daddy. She pried his mouth open and began to pour the sweet mixture into the corner of his crooked mouth. As I watched her on her knees carefully and lovingly tend to him on the floor, I was asking myself another question, "How do you love a monster?" From that day on Mama did not ask me to make the water anymore she asked Eddie to do it.

I asked her once why Daddy drank so much. She said that he did it because his soul was thirsty. The politics of wants and needs were explained away very simply by a thirsty soul. Maybe it was easier to say than to admit that the war raging in him weakened him slowly, hour by hour, from one day-labor line to the next. When I think about it, it was not too difficult to see the weight that he carried. The bulk of the load was in the slump of his shoulders, the dryness of his hands, and the cracks in his chewed up fingernails.

Fatigue quietly rapped itself around Daddy and so, in turn, did the bottle. For My father the pressure of having skin too light to be black or too dark to be white, during times of Malcolm and Martin, made things heavier for him. Inside lay the fear that having a family was more than he could handle, and more than his pride was willing to face. His parched soul was quenched with Wild Irish Rose wine and a predictable explosion whenever he permitted himself to see the truth. I am not sure what his mindset may have been; however, I do think that he lacked the knowledge of a certain reality. He was a husband, and a father who always appeared to be a few dollars away from next to nothing. I used to watch him sit in the chair near the kitchen window, smoking Kool Filter King cigarettes back to back.

The smoke spewed from his lips and changed from misshaped circles to rolling whispers of a mist. He smoked so much that I could not tell whether he was blowing it out, or breathing it in. Calm chaos is what it looked like to me. I would watch and wonder. I wondered if what was stuck inside of him was stuck inside of me. A Doctor Jekyll and Mr. Hyde, caught in a life that he did not want; chain smoking Kool Filter King cigarettes, staring out of a window, a few dollars away from next to nothing and angry at an enemy that he refused to see. Maybe that is why Daddy's soul was so thirsty because he kept quenching it with the wrong things.

On the other hand, Mama was masterful with my brother and me. She creatively caressed our minds with the secrets of crayons, papers and pencils. She changed our little radio into full blown animated concerts, and our bible stories into live red sea performances. She made us forget the aches that no food brought. She used her wit to fill our empty bellies and showered us with so much love that our hearts overflowed. God blessed Mama with the strength and courage of a lioness. To Eddie and me she was the one bit of proof of how much God must love us.

Facing the monster almost every night took a whole lot more than her small mocha frame could handle alone. It required a power that had to be coming straight from God, and her sanctified energy was unmistakable every time the monster came home instead of Daddy. In the kitchen, we could hear glasses crashing and furniture falling; our father was drunk and we knew that we would wake up to Mama's black eyes and bruised skin. When this happened we would turn our attention to the outside world, beyond the thin pale colored center block walls to escape the monster's rage. We would sit quietly in the windowsill and lean our rusty elbows on its edge.

Outside in the playground, just before you reached the busy street, we watched a broken chain link fence sway with the rhythm of the windy city air. Battered steel garbage drums rocked on their sides, and parts of sliding boards leaned helplessly on bent iron legs. Crooked signpost poles lay still on the ground with clumps of concrete still clinging to their base. Scattered trash swirled across a dusty barren earth, mimicking miniature tornadoes. Near a garbage filled sandbox were bits and pieces of what once were swings.

Yet, through it all, and despite the matching red brick gated mountains that hid most of the sky; it was the little specks of shattered, colored glass glimmering in the crevices of cracked sidewalks that always seemed to capture our attention. Sometimes if you watched them closely, and the sun hit them just right, drops of dazzling color would dance. We felt that this daytime performance was only us, and we would let ourselves get lost in it until the monster left, nighttime came, or the streets woke up.

"Rhea?"

"Yeah Eddie."

"You think God see everything?"

"Ma says he does."

Eddie looked at me with wide hopeful eyes and said, "You think he see when Daddy be hitting Mama?"

His question surprised me, but I knew why he felt a need to ask it. I knew what he really wanted to know, he wanted to know if God could see through these mountains and hear the madness. After all, if he could not, it would mean that we had wasted a lifetime in prayers. We fell asleep praying to God, begging for simple stuff; and, the thought of wasted devotion is frightening. God had to know what was going on, how could he not? I know that that was what Eddie dwelled on, but I dwelled on other things like getting, bigger, older, stronger just in case the sights and sounds were out of God's domain. "Yup," I said with as much authority in my voice as I could muster. Eddie turned back to the window, looked up into the sky and added in a whispering voice, "I show hope he can see through these big buildings."

We needed each other just as we needed our window in the mountain when it came time for us to escape. Our closeness is what gave us an inner peace when everything else seemed so hopeless, and when we thought no one else was listening. Eddie and I were linked and fused together to make one seasoned old soul. We were more than brother and sister and more than twins. We were the other half of each other's spirit, shielded by flesh and embedded in bone.

We lived in the middle of a war zone; 514 E. 35th Street Apartment #307 was our world and the window in the mountain was our only view of it. Playtime in the sunshine took place at Grandma's house, away from the projects, away from the danger, and away from the monster. We had to make the most of things with what we could find in our room. Sheets turned into tents, coat hangers wedged into the holes of the radiator, turned into steering wheels; and, one toy turned into many when it was broken apart. The imagination that Mama taught us to use became the gateway to anything and everywhere.

Our favorite games were 'Johnny Lightning' and 'Jack.' We created 'Johnny Lightning' because it helped us clean up our room. Sometimes Daddy would stand in our bedroom doorway and shake his heads at us while using his, "I mean business" baritone voice,

"Boy, boy, boy. You' all got four minutes to clean up this room." We did not know what "four minutes," was, but we knew that we had to clean up our room in a flash. One of us would yell out, 'Johnny Lightning', which meant move as fast as you possibly could. I imagined myself moving like the Speedy Gonzales cartoon character leaving a trail of smoke behind me.

The clothes that were on the floor went into the closet; our toys went with them or under the bed, and trash went under the rug. Once we put a cover over ruffled sheets, it all appeared to be neat. Now, I cannot say if we cleaned our junky room in four minutes, but I can say that when Mama or Daddy came in to check on us they would nod their heads with approval and walk away.

Now the game of 'Jack' was our version of a fantasy game. There were no board pieces, no funny named characters, no deck of cards to pull from, only a vivid imagination needed to play. The one rule of the game was that everyone's name had to be Jack. Jack was an imaginary fellow that could be anything; and, we acted out our fantasies through him.

You could be Jack spaceman, Jack policeman, Jack fireman. It did not matter, just as long as it had the name Jack in front of it. Eddie and I came close to blows when he tried to convert my playful illusion from Jack into Jacqueline. At first, it did not bother me until he started to suggest the sort of jobs that Jacqueline might have. His suggestions were jobs like a waitress, cashier, secretary, or a nurse. When I asked him why I had to be called Jacqueline and not Jack, his response was almost as bad as the dresses that I wore.

"Because you are a girl and girls don't do those jobs, boys do." His answer infuriated me and made me flash back to the word healer and Mama's battle cry, "You are a damn girl!" I felt heat rise up in my face and my hands curl into a fist. The last thing that I thought I would ever have to do is battle with him just like I battled with Mama. Didn't he know me like he knew himself? All I could do was get angry at my inability to make him understand what I could not explain.

"Don't call me that." I told him in the strongest tone that I could possibly use without yelling. He turned from his task of making a steering wheel from a coat hanger and looked into my piercing eyes. It only lasted for a second before he said, "Don't call you what?" I wanted to say, "Don't call me a girl!" but instead, I said, "Don't call me Jacqueline."

"Ok." Then he shrugged his shoulders and turned back to the radiator. It took a while but my hands uncurled and coolness returned to my face. I did not want to fight with him and the idea that I had no words to give him other than, "Don't call me Jacqueline," saddened me. With one long breathe I let the anger go and became Jack the racecar driver. I made motor sounds and pit stops with a twisted coat hanger on an imaginary race track. From that point on I decided that if I was going to imagine anything, I was not going to squander my energy on dreams that I did not want.

Lesson

We spent a lot of time window watching, playing Jack and waiting for Mama to come home. When it started to get dark outside we would listen carefully to hear her keys in the door. This day we heard the key clink inside the lock and ran to the door barely able to contain our excitement. The door swung open, our faces dropped and we took a few quick steps back, it was Daddy. We stopped in front of him motionless, waiting, waiting to see what kind of mood he brought home. He closed the door behind him and turned his tall dust-covered paint peppered body toward us.

"Where's your Mama?" He asked.

"I don't know," I said softly and shrugged my shoulders.
He took his sweat stained baseball cap off and wiped his face with the
back of his hand; then reached inside his front pants pocket and pulled out
a fist full of change.

"Here," he said as he handed me a few coins, "Go on down to the
candy truck and get me some red licorice; get you all something too."

I hesitated for a moment and thought about what Mama said. She
said that Daddy should not have any sweets, because sugar made his blood
bad. But the thought of that ran in and out of my mind just as quickly as
the idea of candy pushed into it. I grabbed the money and ran out the door.
Candy sure sounded a whole lot better than the sugar and syrup
sandwiches that Eddie and I had been eating. I did not wait for the
elevator; it never ran right anyway. So I took the stairs. There was no way
I was about to miss a chance for something sweet because I was stuck in a
stinky elevator.

The stairs felt gooey under my shoes and they made that smacking
sound every time I lifted my foot up. You know the kind of sound that a

peanut butter and jelly sandwich makes when you pull the bread apart? Well, my shoes made that noise as I tore down that dim lit stairwell like a bat out of hell. I ignored the multicolored smears that covered the walls. I ignored the layer upon layer of caked on filth, because the reward for running such a gauntlet was just a few more steps away.

When I got to the end of the stairwell, the half-hinged exit door was wide open. I could hear the ruckus going on outside. The sound of feet pounding, shuffling, skipping, and running along the fractured pavement recoiled against the cement walls that faded off into an echo. Either the old man was here, or they were gangbanging again. Nevertheless, I stepped out into the thick of things, allowing my strong desire for candy to muffle the alarms going off inside my head.

I could see mothers and fathers hanging from their windows. They hollered out their orders and threw down pieces of money-filled tissue to children eagerly waiting below. Yeah, the old man was here all right because the candy truck is the only thing that I knew could make toilet paper rain from the sky. A twisted coat hanger, extended from where the antenna should be, marked the candy truck's spot. Thick black smoke spewed from the back of this rusted red and white-striped vehicle. The motor was always left running because fights would sometimes break out over who was next, or the police would show up. None of that seemed to matter, though, because people surrounded it and cramped themselves in tightly against its doors so tightly that it rocked from time to time.

Everybody pushed, shoved, and jockeyed for a place in line that would get him or her to the front quicker. We all wanted to get to the side door where the old man and his wife rushed to fill everybody's orders. It was so hard being little. Everyone was so much bigger and stronger than me. I bounced around a pack of people like a ping-pong ball. The smell of the smoke sickened me, but I hung in there. I pushed and yelled like everybody else because we all knew that there were no candy stores or pop machines in our neighborhood.

The old man was our treat shop and the Willy Wonka of the ghetto. Rain or shine, day in and day out, he waited patiently in a project parking lot for money filled paper to drip from high above. He had to recognize that he provided an important service, otherwise why would he show up in a black suit on the same day that he buried his one and only son? No one was arrested for the murder, and in the pits of his sorrow; nothing could stop him from making his afternoon candy run. He served a place that still had the stains of his son's blood splattered on a nearby street, and everyday after that he had to consider if the hands that he took change from were also the hands that took his son's life.

The candy man had to know that his treats meant more to us than candy, and when his son died. There were no doubts about it in anyone's minds that his wares were sugars filled with hopes and dreams for those unable to find any of their own. The empty wrappers that littered the ground were reminders of his celebratory visits that you could take with you long after he was gone. I liked the old man. He always smiled at me and he saw no difference between pop bottles, bottle caps, or food stamps. "They are all 'spendables,' he would say."

I found a spot near the back of the pack and worked my way up to the front. It took forever to get there and I had to squeeze my way to the side door where all transactions took place. I was excited, my heart pounded and I could feel the rhythm of it beat against the warm coins in my hands. I caught the old man's attention and he smiled at me, but somewhere in the midst of it he stopped.

A switch went off inside of him and his eyes grew glossy and red. A quiet washed over the crowd around me and the air seemed to stop, but I paid no attention to the abrupt change, I was next and that was the only thing that mattered. As I began to fix my mouth to call out my favorites, a heavy hand came down hard on my shoulder. The feel of its foreign fingers were insistent and chilling as if straight from a freezer. I let my eyes trace the hand from the tips of its dirty fingernails to an empty space where a pinky finger should be, and then I looked up at him. His face was covered by a red handkerchief and rivers of sweat streamed down the middle of his forehead. It left a trail of liquid that flowed into his wild oversized eyes.

I wanted to say, "Hey, its my turn!" but before I could, he gripped my shoulder tighter and pushed me out of the way like a piece of furniture that needed to be rearranged.

"Gimmie the money." His voice was a low rumble that only the old man and I could hear. Then the stranger pulled a gun from underneath a bleach eaten tee-shirt and pointed it straight at the old man's head. The silver metal was on fire and it flickered in the sunlight. The old man leaned back and reached around his panic stricken wife, who had stepped behind him and knocked over a jar of tootsie rolls. With fumbling hands, he picked up the makeshift register, a swisher sweets cigar box and held it out to him.

The stranger yanked it from him and tucked it under a damp armpit. He was not satisfied with that and wanted more. With one swift swipe he bashed the glowing metal against the side of the old man's balding head. The color rouge oozed over his patchy, crinkled, gray pepper hair. He braced himself against the arms of his now uncontrollably hysterical wife and said, "All right, alright, please don't hurt anyone else with that thing!" Then, he reached inside the crotch of his pants, pulled out a clear plastic bag filled with small white packets and handed it to him.

"Here, take it and go."

They made a clear path for the stranger and no one looked up at him, no one tried to stop him, and no one said a word. For me time stood still, and in that moment I learned just how long a second could be. I saw the old man's wife's tears stream down into the wrinkled lines of her cheeks. She dabbed at her husband's gaping wound with the corners of her blue cotton dress and cried out to Jesus a few times. I stood in front of them curious. I was not sure of what was going on. What kind of candy was this that caused strangers to make old men bleed? The old man's voice cut through the fog of my thoughts, and I struggled to hear him over the bells ringing in my ears. He looked at me with great care, gently placed his hand on my shoulder, and in a tender soothing sweet soft sound said, "Now what can I get for you today, baby?"

The experience tugged at my mind and made me search for words that I had not yet learned. Rewinding in my mind were the images of red rivers flowing down the sides of the old man's face; the steadiness of the stranger's hand; the glisten of the silver metal and the hush of the crowd behind. All would remain in my mind forever.

I sat in the window of our bedroom chewing on Mary Janes and apple flavored Now Laters, reliving the events of the day. By the time the last Mary Jane was gone I had decided that I was going to hold onto those pictures. I was going to hold onto them until I could find a language to describe them and maybe after that they would fade away.

We got up extra early on school days because if you could get to the lunchroom before 8:30 you could have as many bowls of oatmeal and cartons of milk that your stomach could hold. For some strange reason that I could never figure out, some of the other kids played with their food. They spent breakfast time drawing trails through their oatmeal and turning up their noses at anyone who actually ate it. Some of them had a serious indignation for the food that lay in front of them, and it made me wonder if hunger was a pain that only Eddie and I were susceptible to feeling.

Doolittle East was not much to look at. Something about Doolittle mirrored a castle. Its tall chimneystacks, long slender smoky windows, and perfectly lined yellow bricks surrounded by a well-kept lawn reminded me of the houses that I had seen in fairytales. It was a big school and very strict. When entering the building and exiting, the boys and girls were separated and had to use different doors. Going up the steps, you stayed to the right, and going down the steps, you stayed to the right. There was no gum chewing allowed and no bathroom breaks until the teacher said so. Moreover, if you did not mind your manners or talked back, you went straight to the Principal's office. The office is where they made calls to parents for permission to use the paddle on you.

Mr. Harper was our Principal and during the morning bells, you could see him walking down the center of the hallways in a slow ceremonial military style. He barely moved his head as he passed the usual morning greeters. For the most part students stayed clear of him as his presence was always a cause for alarm. The dread was hard to notice at first, but after a while you could see it peeking out through the hustle and bustle of the day. Mr. Harper was a tall, slender cream-colored man who would seem under any other ordinary circumstances to blend in with the melee. His brown suit and neatly knotted black tie did not make him stand out more than any other adult; however, there was something about him, and that something was in the deliberate methodical march that he graced the hallways with each day.

The one who made the call when it came time for the paddling was Mr. Harper. All you had to do was look at the way children avoided him. It was easy to pick out the kids that had been stung by the paddle's wooden bite. In many cases, they would be the ones running into the classrooms as if their pants were on fire. No quick hellos or slanted smiles, just small bodies trying to move in the opposite direction. For most of the students, it never could be an ordinary day, and Mr. Harper was not some partial blur in their peripheral vision. He was the hustle and the bustle, and the reason why children cried when sent his way.

The paddle had given him what some parents and teachers called a knack for discipline, but what it really gave him was a smile full of smirk that could inflict real pain. He was confident that once permission was given, he could invoke an avalanche of obedience, and all with a fateful glance. I witnessed this talent for terror first hand. My teacher sent me to the Principal's office for doodling in a History class. I was a part of my scribble, I was the flock of black birds in the middle of the page. My wings stretched out over snow-covered mountains and iced-over treetops. No sooner had I captured the wind under my feathers when Mrs. Dotson's heavy teacher's book came crashing down onto the top of my desk. Sheets of notebook paper flew into the air and the roar of it snatched me out of my flight and hurled me into her big brown weeping eyes.

Her round-nosed, dark-skinned face was shadowed with anguish. She began to tell me about how my people marched so that I could sit in class that day. She told me about people attacked with water hoses and dogs, billy clubs, and bats; how our ancestors died in ships and toiled over cotton just so I could sit with my doodles and scribble my life away. She went on and on, point by point, passionately, tearfully drilling into me every bit of black sacrifice that she could name.

When she was done, I was out of breath, not because I had anything to say, not because I had run a marathon, but because I suddenly felt ashamed. I waited outside the Principal's office with another kid. He fiddled around anxiously in his chair, as he knew what was coming. I could see that he was scared and his fear made it difficult for him to stay still. The anxiety inside of him built up and bubbled into slow quiet tears. His tears became a steady flow when we were both lead into the back office where Mr. Harper sat waiting in his big lime green leather chair. He called my mother first and I felt a panic rush through me.

I felt the kind of panic that grows inside of you so fast that you do not notice it until it reaches your knees. There was no window for me to daydream my fear into nothingness. I looked down and stared at my feet, forcing myself to bury the fear where no one could find it, not even me. I chewed on my fingernails as Mr. Harper pressed the phone to his ear and let his fingers spin around the dial.

Somehow, I knew that Mama would never allow it. She had risked too much of her own wellbeing to protect me, and there was no way in hell she was going to relinquish that duty because a voice on the phone said so. She did not care how well he spoke or how insistent he was, this was her child, her cross to bear and she would die a thousand lifetimes before she gave up that right. Bottom line, if there was going to be any lickings to pass out, she would be the one delivering them, and not some fancy talking know-it-all on the phone. Mama was firm with him, and I could tell because of Mr. Harper's tight jaws and cream-colored skin that had now turned red.

"Yes, Ms. Thomason I heard you. No one is going to put their hands on your child, Madam."

His slight southern drawl was calm yet it cracked a little and in my mind's eye I could see the expression on my Mama's face as she yelled out, "No one's going to put their hands on my child but me!" When he replaced the phone back onto the receiver, his lips had rolled up as if he could not bear the taste of his own spit. He told me to have a seat next to the globe opposite his desk while he reached inside a top drawer for the paddle. He made me watch his twisted brand of resolve. The boy, whose face was filled with fear, now had pain to match it. I braced myself as I watched and listened to the boy's cries bounce off the walls in a sickening smacking beat every time the paddle met with his backside.

Mama must have hit a nerve with Mr. Harper because he quickly forgot that he had another phone call to make, or was too mad to care. I am sure that he was not used to parents ignoring his professional advice, especially the parents who lived in the nearby projects. Mama's proper tones coupled with naughty nice words troubled him and made him feel small. Whatever she said that bothered him also led him to believe that the only way to regain his credibility was to have me watch him whip that little boy's ass. My panic was gone, he had lost command, and I marveled at his apparent weakness. With one phone call, my Mama peeled away his Teflon layer and exposed his Achilles heel.

In a way, I was grateful for that experience. Sure, I felt bad for the little boy who had gotten his butt whipped, but at the same time, I was happy. I was happy because I would never have to scurry through the hallway when I saw him, I would never know what it was like to cower under his watchful glare. My trip to his office left me with a significant lesson. I learned that words held more power than a paddle, and that if I could master them, they would provide me with another shield of protection. I never went out of my way to remind him of his impotence, but just like his Omni confident stroll, I had a swagger of my own. Mr. Harper's discipline was a fraud, and the awareness of that fact inoculated me against his tyranny.

NOTES

qp

www.ingramcontent.com/pod-product-compliance
Lightning Source LLC
Chambersburg PA
CBHW021303280526
45784CB00005B/2494